THE PERSONAL IMPACT OF NAZI PERSECUTION EXPERIENCES AND LIFE STORIES

by
Mary Fulbrook

The Fourth
Martin Miller and Hannah Norbert-Miller
Memorial Lecture

Research Centre for German and Austrian Exile Studies
INSTITUTE OF MODERN LANGUAGES RESEARCH
School of Advanced Study, University of London

2017

Published by the
INSTITUTE OF MODERN LANGUAGES RESEARCH
School of Advanced Study, University of London
Senate House, Malet Street, London WC1E 7HU

http://www.modernlanguages.sas.ac.uk

ISBN 978 0 85457 264 9

Cover design based on an image kindly
supplied by Anthony Grenville

INTRODUCTION

It is an honour for the Institute of Modern Languages Research, on behalf of the Martin Miller and Hannah Norbert-Miller Trust and the Research Centre for German & Austrian Exile Studies at the Institute, to welcome tonight's speaker on the occasion of the Fourth Martin Miller and Hannah-Norbert Miller Memorial Lecture.

Mary Fulbrook is Professor of German History and Dean of the Faculty of Social and Historical Sciences at University College London. She studied at Newnham College, Cambridge, and at Harvard University, where she was awarded an MA and PhD. She has also held a Harvard Centre for European Studies Krupp Fellowship at the LSE and a Lady Margaret Research Fellowship at New Hall (now Murray Edwards College), Cambridge. She served as Head of Department at UCL between January 1995 and September 2006, and as Vice-Dean of the Faculty of Arts and Humanities for three years, before becoming Executive Dean of the Faculty of Social and Historical Sciences in 2013. A Fellow of the British Academy, she was a member of the British Academy's Council and has chaired its Modern History Section. Professor Fulbrook was the first female Chair of the German History Society and founding Joint Editor of its journal, *German History*, and is currently on the Editorial Board of *German Politics and Society* and other journals.

As will become apparent, Professor Fulbrook's knowledge and research expertise are particularly appropriate for this lecture series: she is a member of the Academic Advisory Board (*wissenschaftliches Kuratorium*) of the Memorial Foundation for the former concentration camps of Buchenwald and Mittelbau-Dora, and a member of the International Advisory Board of the Bundeskanzler-Willy-Brandt-Stiftung. The GDR is one of her research specialisms and in 1995 she published the pioneering *Anatomy of a Dictatorship: Inside the GDR 1949-89*, and *The People's State: East German Society from Hitler to Honecker* in 2005. She has also explored social and historical theory and the legacies of the past in *Historical Theory* (2002) and *German National Identity after the Holocaust* (1999). All in all, Professor Fulbrook is author or editor of more than twenty books, including the best-selling *Concise History of Germany* (CUP, 2nd edn 2002) and *History of Germany 1918-2014: The Divided Nation* (Blackwell, 4th edn 2014). Her most recent publications include *A Small Town near Auschwitz: Ordinary Nazis and the Holocaust* (OUP, 2012), *Dissonant Lives: Generations and Violence through the German Dictatorships* (OUP, 2011), and *Becoming East German: Socialist Structures and Sensibilities after Hitler* (ed. with Andrew Port, 2013). She is currently directing the AHRC-funded research project 'Reverberations of War in Germany and Europe since 1945'. Her forthcoming book, *Reckonings: Legacies of Nazi Persecution* (OUP) explores the continuing significance of experiences of Nazi persecution among perpetrators, victims and members of subsequent generations, material which forms the basis of this evening's lecture.

Martin Miller and Hannah Norbert-Miller were Jewish actors who sought refuge in Britain, going on to brilliant careers in film, theatre and radio. Martin Miller's satirical parodies of Hitler's speeches were broadcast to Germany by the BBC between 1940 and 1942. The Millers are represented here this evening by their son, Daniel, a music producer, who in 1978 founded Mute Records to promote electronic and alternative music, Depeche Mode being one of the notable acts he featured. A self-made man in the world of music and entertainment, Daniel has followed in his parents' footsteps as fine examples of the tremendous contribution made by enterprising refugees to this country's wealth and well-being in business, charity, culture and leisure.

A brief history of the Research Centre for German & Austrian Exile Studies and biography of the Millers follow this Introduction. Thank you all for being here this evening.

Catherine Davies
Director, IMLR

December 2016

THE RESEARCH CENTRE FOR GERMAN & AUSTRIAN EXILE STUDIES AT THE IMLR

The IMLR is the successor to the Institute of Germanic & Romance Studies, established in 2004 with the merger of the Institute of Germanic Studies and the Institute of Romance Studies. The Institute of Romance Studies was founded in 1989, covering French, Italian, Portuguese and Spanish. The Institute of Germanic Studies was founded in 1950, covering the literatures and cultures of the areas in which German and other Germanic languages are spoken.

It was in 1995 that the Research Centre for German & Austrian Exile Studies was established at the then Institute of Germanic Studies, bringing together the London Research Group for German and Austrian Exiles and the Research Centre for Germans and Austrians in Britain at the University of Aberdeen. At the time Hamish Ritchie, Emeritus Professor at the University of Aberdeen and President of the Centre, donated his books on exile to the Institute's Library, forming the mainstay of a growing specialist collection. This has been and continues to be augmented by regular donations of archive material, including the papers of Martin and Hannah Norbert-Miller, and the collection includes a bank of recordings capturing the memories of a very articulate community.

The work of the Centre focuses on the history of German-speaking émigrés who found refuge in this country, on their personal recollections and experiences and on their enrichment of the life of the UK in such varied spheres as the professions, industry and commerce, literature, art and culture, politics, publishing, the media and the world of entertainment and leisure. The Centre's activities include running seminars and conferences on a variety of topics in its field and publishing monographs and collections of essays, as well as the *Yearbook of the Research Centre for German and Austrian Exile Studies* (Leiden: Brill). The Martin Miller and Hannah Norbert-Miller Trust was established in 2009 to support the work of the Centre. It funds bursaries for doctoral study and visiting fellowships at the Institute, as well as providing sponsorship for the Centre's triennial conferences and other projects.

MARTIN MILLER AND HANNAH NORBERT-MILLER

Born in Moravia in 1899, Martin Miller was an actor and cabaret artist in Austria and Czechoslovakia. When he arrived in England in 1939, he spoke little English, and so tended to play the role of 'the foreigner' (sinister conspirators, doctors or the inevitable psychoanalyst). Often these were cameo roles, but they could also be show-stoppers, such as his impersonation of Hitler in *Der Führer spricht*. This party-piece, performed at the *Laterndl* cabaret theatre, happened to be heard by Richard Crossman, the Labour MP, who was at the time Minister for Propaganda, and who invited him to reprise it on 1 April 1940 on the BBC German Service as part of its contribution to the war effort.

A series of stage roles followed: *Arsenic and Old Lace* (playing Dr Einstein), the original production of *The Mousetrap* (playing Mr Paravicini), and Pinter's *The Birthday Party*, to name but a few. During his career he played alongside many of the best-known names of the mid-century, such as Peggy Ashcroft, Dirk Bogarde, Edith Evans, Michael Redgrave and Richard Attenborough, who became a great friend. The list of his film and TV appearances reads like a litany of the British media from the early 1940s to the late 1960s, and included parts in *The Third Man, Exodus, The Pink Panther, Dixon of Dock Green, Dr Who* and *The Forsyte Saga*. He died in 1969 in Austria while filming *The Last Valley*.

Hannah Norbert was already well known as an actress in Austria during the 1930s. She had been touring in the provinces towards the end of that decade when it became impossible for a Jewish actor or actress to get parts. After the *Anschluss*, she left Vienna and went to Paris, from where she sought entry to the UK — and succeeded only at the second attempt. Martin Miller, meanwhile, was in Berlin, and arrived direct from there. Both owe their arrival here in 1939 to the support of the Quakers. I believe they met in London, and married here in 1942.

As is the case with so many of their contemporaries, Hannah and Martin do not just represent the span of the twentieth-century's worst and best moments — the loss of homeland as Hitler exiles, the finding of a new homeland in the UK —, they are also part of its cultural richness, its performance: from theatre and cabaret to film and TV as these grew into prominence (without leaving the other media quite behind). It is to their son, Daniel Miller, himself a major figure in the UK entertainment industry, music producer and the founder of Mute Records, who has worked both here and in Europe (especially Berlin), that we owe the generous donation in his parents' name.

Naomi Segal

February 2011 IGRS Director, 2004-2011

THE PERSONAL IMPACT OF NAZI PERSECUTION
EXPERIENCES AND LIFE STORIES[1]

The experience of surviving Nazi persecution had an impact on the whole of the rest of people's lives. It had a massive impact on the transformation of people's identities. But the character of this impact, and the stories people told about their lives, varied not only according to their age, status and experiences at the time of persecution but also according to later circumstances in which they sought to make new lives. The impact on the 'second' and subsequent generations similarly varied not only with parental experiences but also with the different contexts in which children grew up. In other words, the vast and rich psychological literature on the consequences of Nazi persecution for individuals, and the literary analyses of texts in the light of theories of trauma, need to be complemented by historical exploration of how particular post-war contexts affected the ways in which people gave significance and expression to their memories of the past. This is an enormous field of inquiry, and here I can only sketch a few outlines of some key issues and aspects.

For all who were affected by Nazi persecution, there was an impact in terms of the transformation of identity: a transformation from the person and the life that might have been, to the person and the life they had to

1 Lecture given on Thursday, 1 December 2016. This lecture draws on material and arguments from my book on *Reckonings: Legacies of Nazi Persecution* (Oxford University Press, forthcoming), the research for which was generously supported by a grant from the AHRC for a collaborative project on 'Reverberations of War in Germany and Europe since 1945'.

make under quite different and often entirely unforeseen and unpredicted circumstances. This transformation in identity is encapsulated beautifully in a joke about a Yiddish-speaking survivor with a near unpronounceable eastern European name. On the boat to the USA, with the assistance of friends with a better command of English, he had arduously rehearsed the anglicised spelling and pronunciation he was planning to give to the immigration officials at Ellis Island. Arriving in New York, however, he became disorientated in the throngs crowding the hall, and when his turn came and the immigration official barked out the request for his name, he confusedly lapsed into Yiddish, saying that he had 'already forgotten': 'shoyn fargesn – schon vergessen'. Without looking up or asking for spelling, the official noted down the survivor's name as he had heard it: 'Shaun Ferguson'. From then on, in his new life this Eastern European Jew had to live with an imposed identity and associated assumptions on the part of all he met that seemed improbably far from any reality. He may well have severely disappointed the local Irish-American communities who had assumed from his name that he would be 'one of them'.

The story may be apocryphal, and we will not try to imagine Shaun Ferguson's future life any further. But it does point up the sharpness of the break between 'before' and 'after', and the significance of the transition from one life to another. Here, I shall explore just some of the variations in people's experiences and the ways in which they were subsequently challenged, constrained or invited to produce particular stories of their lives – or how they chose to represent themselves to selected others, at different times in their lives. I will also briefly consider some of the implications for subsequent generations and for historical research today.

In discussing this topic, I will roughly distinguish between accounts given by those who were able to escape from Nazi persecution before war and genocide engulfed Europe, and those who remained on the continent during the war, most of whom died, but some of whom survived. The terminology for these different groups is not uncontroversial. Those who managed to get out before the war are variously referred to as 'émigrés', 'exiles', or 'refugees'; those who managed to write about their experiences on the continent during the war but then perished before the end of Nazi rule are seen as 'victims'; and those who not only managed to live through but also long enough after the end of the war eventually came to be called 'survivors'.

We can use these terms analytically, for purposes of distinguishing different types of experience of persecution; but it should be noted that, over the decades, these terms have also become loaded with emotional and evaluative weightings. 'Hierarchies of victimhood' emerged, even for those still exposed to Nazi persecution in wartime. At times it appeared as if only people who had survived the very worst of the camps 'truly' deserved the term 'survivors', whereas those who had somehow got out before or during the war, or had eked out an existence in less well-known labour camps or in hiding, were not quite of the same order of victimhood. Even among camp survivors, those with the Auschwitz tattoo on their arm were somehow assumed to be 'superior' to those who had 'only' experienced other camps. Additionally, among all groups there were differences based not only on personal characteristics such as social status, religious beliefs, gender and age, but also on the Nazi grounds for persecution. There have accordingly been bitter debates about whether Roma and Sinti ('gypsies') have the same status as Jews, or about whether the attempted Nazi 'Final Solution of the Jewish Question' was a historical event of a quite different order from the persecution of gay men, Jehovah's Witnesses, people with mental and physical disabilities, so-called 'a-socials', and other victims of Nazi violence. Even when there is broad moral agreement that every death at the hands of the Nazis was a murder that should not have happened, some insist that there is not merely a quantitative but also a qualitative difference in the fate of Jews: in the Nazi worldview, Jews were in principle designated for death simply by virtue of existing.

It is worth then saying explicitly at the outset: for purposes of historical precision, it is important to be aware of distinctions between the experiences of different groups among the victims of Nazi persecution. But this does not mean that the sufferings of different groups should be evaluated, compared, and placed on some spurious moral scale of a hierarchy of victimhood and degrees of suffering. The pain and the tragedy of persecution in the catastrophe that engulfed Europe under Nazi rule affected people massively, even if in different ways. For all the differences in detail, experiences of stigmatisation, humiliation, degradation, and for many also the ever-present threat of death, meant that there was a massive gulf between those who were persecuted and those who were 'on the side of the perpetrators'. One can then, in the broadest brush, speak of contrasting 'communities of experience'.

All of these features make it very difficult to talk of 'survivors' as though this were an unproblematic term. There were not only many different reasons why people were persecuted, but also different perceptions of these groups both at the time and later. The life stories that people recounted therefore depended not only on personal experiences at the time, but also on degrees of sympathy and receptivity among later audiences for particular kinds of victims and certain kinds of story. The stories of many who did not conform to an expected narrative were never elicited at all; if offered, they tended to be marginalised or ignored, excluded from published selections, overlooked in discussions of 'survivor testimony'.

If agreeing a terminology for the persecuted is difficult, defining those on the side of the perpetrators is arguably even harder, and the variations in their stories far less easily encapsulated. The Nazification of German and

Austrian society (and of European societies more broadly) affected all who lived through this period, including those who were direct perpetrators and those who are often, inadequately and problematically, termed 'bystanders'. In comparison with the stories of survivors, the voices of those who were complicit with the Nazi system have barely been analysed, largely considered not to be 'testimonies', and, at the extreme, deemed to be mainly a matter of cover-ups and denials. Yet without the actions and inaction of members of the majority society, mass persecution could not have taken place on the scale that it did.

I will start with some reflections on the question of time, looking both at the significance of the time of talking or writing about the past, and at the ways in which the times of personal lives interrelated with historical time. I will then go on to look at how people portrayed former social relations and later identities. I will also, briefly, consider some of the more difficult aspects of narratives about this deeply difficult past, one that it was impossible to live through without coming out in some way tainted.

I. The Time of Telling

The time of telling life stories made a difference, even within any similar group. I will distinguish between several phases of accounts.

(a) Before the War

The kinds of story told in 1939 or 1940, before the Nazi policies for 'final solution of the Jewish question' had come into full force, and that can be found in the fascinating collection of essays solicited under the title 'My Life in Germany before and after 1933' (held in the Harvard Houghton

Library), differ from accounts given during or after the war.[2] At this point, having left Germany but not yet settled in new environments, many of those whose essays were collected by the Harvard professors were in what has been termed 'suspended identities': they found themselves in new places largely through chance rather than choice, yet they had been forced to sever all ties with their previous homelands and had no certainty about which family members or friends they would ever see again.[3] For them, at this point, the biggest break in their lives was either 1933, for those who had lived in Germany, or 1938, for those who came from Austria and where the Nazi *Anschluss* of March proved the decisive turning point in their lives. The 'new lives' were still precarious, uncertain; émigrés faced futures that they could neither imagine nor predict. The writers' impressions of the rapid changes that had taken place in their lives since the Nazi takeover in their home country – whether in 1933 or 1938 – were very fresh and immediate; their perceptions of any possible future were wide open, largely unimaginable. Some indeed wrote out of sheer desperation, in the hope that the Harvard professors would be able to extend something by way of help, whether in the form of financial assistance or affidavits and names of people who could provide practical support in their plight. Certainly the prospect of a financially significant prize played a role in the willingness of many to provide an account, in the hope of gaining the wherewithal to build a future of sorts. Some, however, would face no future at all. There are a few heart-breaking

---

2 These remarks are largely based on the collection of essays under the title 'My Life in Germany before and after 1933' held in the Harvard Houghton Library (hereafter HHL).

3 Harry Liebersohn and Dorothee Schneider, 'Editors' Introduction', *My Life in Germany before and after January 30, 1933*. A Guide to a Manuscript Collection at Houghton Library, Harvard University (Philadelphia: American Philosophical Society, 2001), p. 6.

submissions from people still trapped in Europe, even if no longer in Germany, and from whom the traces were subsequently lost.

So what were, for these writers on the brink of war, the biggest changes that had taken place in their lives? For those people of Jewish descent who lived in Germany, the changes in their own personal status and in informal interpersonal relationships over a relatively short period loomed very large. A few dwelt at length on their experiences as children or young people in Imperial Germany and in the Weimar Republic. Men who were already middle aged or older had often fought in the First World War, and could barely believe how little their comradeship in arms of that time now seemed to count. People who had been among the educated classes, including university professors, civil servants, and schoolteachers now found that 'race' was more important than 'class', as they lost established social and professional positions. The most painful experiences for many of these writers – whatever their age and social status – were the ways in which former friends suddenly dropped their friendship, and acquaintances and neighbours shunned or ignored them if meeting by chance on the streets or in public places. Parents feared also for the future of their children, given adverse experiences in school and the closure of certain career paths to them. This was, notably, also the case for 'mixed marriage' families, where the children were what the Nazis termed *Mischlinge*, or persons of mixed descent. These children seem often to have been treated as badly by schoolteachers, by people in charge of apprenticeships and training schemes, and by potential employers, as those of fully Jewish descent, irrespective of the fine details of the Nuremberg Laws. Family relationships were strained, with the 'Aryan' spouse often under massive pressure – from friends and family as well as state authorities – to divorce the Jewish partner. In some tragic cases, the Jewish parent committed suicide, in the hope that despite the private tragedy this would make things easier for their loved ones. It also seems to have been relatively rare that an 'Aryan' person who was not yet married chose to stick with an intimate partner of Jewish descent.

In a myriad of ways, both officially instigated and on an informal everyday level, it becomes clear from these accounts just how much 'ordinary Germans' participated in creating two quite different communities of experience: those who were marginalised and persecuted, and those who were not. Historiographical debates over coercion and consent, over the relative roles of enthusiasm and fear, and the significance of the growing apparatus of terror as well as 'what people knew', would do well to take into account also these striking behavioural changes that were effected often apparently spontaneously or through informal social processes on the ground.[4]

As far as physical violence was concerned, the experiences of *Kristallnacht* in November 1938 and, for many adult males, subsequent incarceration in a concentration camp, loomed very large. This was, it seemed to those writing in the autumn of 1939 or the early months of 1940, the worst the persecution of the Jews could get. For Austrian writers in this collection, the *Anschluss* of March 1938 immediately inaugurated a period of

4 These and the following paragraphs are based on reading accounts in the Harvard Houghton Library archive collection. See also the published selections in Uta Gerhardt and Thomas Karlauf (eds), *The Night of Broken Glass: Eyewitness Accounts of Kristallnacht* (Cambridge: Polity Press, 2012, transl. by Robert Simmons and Nick Somers); Margarete Limberg and Herbert Rübsaat (eds), *Sie durften nicht mehr Deutsche sein: Jüdischer Alltag in Selbstzeugnissen 1933-1938* (Frankfurt/New York: Campus Verlag, 1990), with a reduced selection of these in English translation in Margarete Limberg and Hubert Rübsaat, *Germans no more. Accounts of Jewish Everyday Life, 1933-38* (New York and Oxford: Berghahn, 2006; transl. by Alan Nothnagle); Margarete Limberg and Hubert Rübsaat (eds), *Nach dem 'Anschluss'. Berichte österreichischer EmigrantInnen aus dem Archiv der Harvard University* (Vienna: Mandelbaum Verlag, 2013).

heightened fear, exacerbated only too soon by the physical violence of 9-10 November 1938. Many were almost immediately embroiled in the lengthy and difficult process of attempting to gain visas to emigrate.

Interestingly, a few writers at this time still held out hope for those they had left behind. In some cases, indeed, the authors of the essays had left well before their partners or children, in the hope and expectation that they would then be able to follow some months later. There was as yet little or nothing that would warrant the term, later so frequently applied, of 'survivor guilt'. People did not at this time know what might be the fates of those who had 'not yet' escaped from persecution. The greatest personal impact of persecution at this point was arguably on sense of identity and life course. All had over a period of years or months prior to their departure suffered the forcible loss of social status; all had faced difficult questions about when, where, even whether they should try to consort with former friends; all had to make decisions about how they should adjust their activities, deal with their possessions and relationships, and try to steer the future course of their lives. While many were already aware of their distinct status as a member of a minority religious and social group, others suddenly had an identity thrust upon them that had not previously been relevant in any way. This was the case with, for example, people of Jewish descent who were not themselves professing Jews (whether because they were Christians or non-believers). It was also, in varying ways, the case for people of mixed descent – the so-called *Mischlinge* – who found themselves suddenly discriminated against and in effect doubly excluded as being neither 'Jewish' nor 'Aryan'. All had one key aspect of their identity radically affected: the capacity not only to define oneself, but also to have realistic aspirations for a relatively predictable future. They faced highly uncertain circumstances, in which personal capacities and previous plans, hopes and expectations for the future course of their lives became entirely irrelevant. Those who had been able to get out before the war and were able to write while on the brink of new lives register the sense of being on a cliff edge, with no idea about what path to follow once they had got away from the brink. A few we are able to trace and find out about the later lives they had managed to lead, often with surprising success; the traces of many others are lost.[5]

(b) During the War

The testimonies of those who wrote during the war about what was happening to themselves and their communities are of quite a different character, and have been widely analysed and used by historians. Testimonies written during the war vary greatly in character and purpose, from the diaries of teenagers such as Mary Berg in the Warsaw ghetto – who, belonging to a wealthy family with an American mother, was able to get out to the USA – or Dawid Sierakowiak and others in the Łódź ghetto, or Rutka Laskier in Będzin, through the sober reflections and notes of people like Adam Czerniaków, or the circles around Emanuel Ringelblum in Warsaw, or the chronicles of the Łódź ghetto dwellers, to individual accounts such as that by Szlamek, an escapee from Chełmno

---

5 Those whose subsequent lives I have been able to follow, by virtue of their successful pursuit of professional activities following emigration, include: Robert Breusch, HHL, b MS Ger 91 (38); 'John Hay' (pseudonym), HHL, b MS Ger 91 (89); Victor Paschkis, HHL, b MS Ger 91 (176), who in the USA became a Quaker and professor at Columbia University (http://www.nytimes.com/1991/06/20/obituaries/victor-paschkis-93-a-retired-professor-and-pacifist-is-dead.html);. One or two of the HHL writers went on to publish their accounts, including for example Karl Löwith, *My Life in Germany before and after 1933. A Report* (Urbana and Chicago: University of Illinois Press, 1994, transl. by Elizabeth King; orig. German 1986).

who sought to bring news of this first death camp to the outside world, and many others.[6]

The predominant focus of many of these accounts is simply on trying to survive, and to understand what is happening while the war and the waves of persecution were still in process – and while there might yet be ways out or alternative ways forwards. Whether recounting family scenes, as people's behaviour changed and tensions mounted, or discussing wider events of the day, these accounts provide immediate insights into the extraordinary difficulty of responding to the overwhelming violence that was engulfing these communities.

One of the most difficult aspects of this period is that of the ways in which some people sought to survive in almost impossible circumstances. Victims of Nazi persecution faced what Lawrence Langer has notably termed 'choiceless choices'. There are very few candid accounts by people who operated in what Primo Levi called 'the grey zone'. In this context, there is just one account from the time of persecution that I want to discuss explicitly, because it treats so directly and with such agonised immediacy the closely related questions of 'coerced complicity' and 'survivor guilt'. In this case, the writer did not survive the war; and the guilt that he felt is recorded so close to the events in question that it provides in heightened and highly articulate form crucial insights into what many people later relayed only more mutedly, buffered perhaps by years of reflection and barriers of self-defensiveness.

---

6 Berg, Mary, Warsaw Ghetto: *A Diary* (New York: L.B. Fischer, 1945; ed. by S.L. Shneiderman); *The Diary of Dawid Sierakowiak, Five Notebooks from the* Łódź *Ghetto* (New York and Oxford: OUP, 1996; ed. and intro. by Alan Adelson).

This account was written during the war by Calel Perechodnik.[7] He was a Jewish policeman in the ghetto of Otwack, thinking that this role would save him from being taken away to labour service and allow him to support his wife and two-year-old child. He initially thought that the war would be relatively brief, that the Germans would soon be defeated, and that working as a member of the ghetto police force would help to protect his wife and young daughter. Entitled *Am I a Murderer?* by the editor and translator, picking up on a sentence in one of the most agonised passages in the book, Perechodnik's account provides an extraordinary combination of bitter, incisive analysis of the mentalities of Jews, Poles, and Germans, as their interactions during the period of occupation transformed all of them. Far from being passive in face of their impending fate, but not knowing what strategies might work, what rumours to believe, what courses of action might have what outcomes, it was almost impossible for Jews to know what choices to make. This was for people in the situation of Perechodnik not so much a matter of 'choiceless choices' as of facing innumerable possible alternatives with no way of knowing what might or might not be successful – and fearing that virtually all actions were unlikely to assist in escaping almost certain death in the machinery of extermination. Perechodnik is himself racked with a sense of guilt, of feeling that he had caused the deaths of his beloved wife and child by mistaken decisions and failures to take certain courses of action when there might still have been some chance of saving them. His wife had

7 Calel Perechodnik, *Am I a Murderer? Testament of a Jewish Ghetto Policeman* (Boulder, Colorado: Westview Press, 1996; ed. and transl. by Frank Fox). For selective omissions and distortions in the published Polish version and related English translation, see David Engel, 'On the Bowdlerisation of a Holocaust Testimony: The Wartime Journal of Calek Perechodnik', *Polin*, vol. 12, 1999, pp. 316-329.

begged him to obtain for her an identity pass that might have allowed her to live undetected on the Polish side; she had begged him to leave her and their child hiding in the cellar of their house during the time of the round-up; but he had believed that as the family of a policemen they would be safer coming with him to the round-up site. He was proved bitterly wrong. He had also left it too late to find someone who would be willing to adopt their daughter and bring her up as a Polish Christian – an arrangement was offered just a couple days after they had been deported and gassed. So Perechodnik felt deeply, desperately, guilty and responsible for their deaths – deaths that he felt he might have been able to prevent, had he chosen differently. While he is well aware that the main burden of guilt lay with the Germans, assisted by the callousness and greed of many local Poles, and was also conscious of the enormous difficulty of knowing of any way of surviving in this hostile wider environment, he is still agonised by the fact that he failed to act at crucial moments when he still might have been able to save his wife and child, and that he made the wrong choices. His account is one long scream of remorse, written as much to unburden his own soul as to provide an analysis of what had happened.

(c) The Aftermath: Phases of Post-War Accounts

Life stories given in the immediate aftermath of the war, such as the interviews given to Central Jewish Historical Commission (ZIH) in Poland and similar organisations elsewhere, or the oral history interviews in DP camps recorded by David Boder, were quite different in character. For them the key break in their lives had not been 1933 or 1938, but rather the moment of Nazi invasion during the war, with the sudden entrance of physical violence into their everyday lives, expropriation of their property, expulsion from their homes, moments of deportation to ghettoes or camps. In these interviews there is little or no discussion of slowly changing social relationships among former friends and neighbours in peacetime; the focus is rather on sudden instances of brutality, abrupt interruptions of routines, forcible separation from homes, family and friends; these are disjointed narratives made up of a string of adverse experiences, specific misfortunes and lucky escapes. Unlike those written in 1939-40, these early post-war accounts dwell less on the dissolving intricacies of previous lives than on chronologies of disruption. The stories are sometimes hard to piece together, and often lack any coherent framework of interpretation or wider narrative picture. Interestingly, those that conformed least well to the kinds of narratives that later came to be 'expected' were omitted from later published selections from these interviews.

During the decades of the 1960s and 1970s, when survivors were asked to come forward to provide evidence for Nazi trials, witnesses were primarily expected to provide accounts of the crimes of others, not testify to the effects on themselves. Sometimes termed the 'era of the witness', these decades were certainly not the 'era of the survivor'. That concept only began to emerge from the mid to later 1970s, with the growing interest in oral history, the history of everyday life, and the beginnings of the collection of testimony.

The 'age of the survivor' has lasted until now. From the 1970s, the concentration in testimonies began to be not so much on what survivors had witnessed with respect to the actions of others – the perpetrators – but rather on what had been the effects of persecution on victims. This was the case even in the spate of trials that followed the Demjanjuk case. In the trial of Oskar Groening, for example, witnesses who had never met or seen him were able to testify to the effects on themselves and their families of the deaths of relatives who had been at Auschwitz at the same time as Groening, irrespective of any bearing such testimony might have on proving his personal guilt. The focus broadened to the survivor's whole life.

Even so, there were marked variations in how this took place. The character of these later life stories differed significantly according to the purposes of inquiry and the character of the collection. It is noticeable, for example, that the filmed interviews in the Fortunoff Archive at Yale University allow interviewees to spend proportionately as much time as they like on different periods of their lives. So while the account of the period of persecution may in some cases dominate, in other interviews it is comparatively brief, while the post-war period and later difficulties in dealing with past experiences gain far more space. Interviews carried out by the USC Shoah foundation ('Spielberg archive'), by contrast, generally pre-allot relative proportions of time to be spent on the periods of 'before', 'during' and 'after'.

Written accounts and memoirs differ not only according to the time and the conditions under which they were produced, but also the extent to which survivors were given assistance in writing the memoirs. It is notable that in recent years there has been a spate of publications telling life stories with the assistance of ghost writers, often with the effect of conveying a harrowing personal story in a curiously dispassionate voice, and with somewhat jarring interjections about the wider historical developments at any given time in a personal story.

The time of telling has another and highly significant consequence too – and that is changing receptivity to different kinds of stories, and a related expansion of the category of victimhood. The published sources for 'survivor testimony' tend overwhelmingly to focus on Jewish victims of persecution.[8] But there were many other groups who were persecuted, including people of mixed backgrounds or partially Jewish descent (*Mischlinge*), Roma and Sinti, homosexual men, 'a-socials', political prisoners, forced labourers, and people suffering from mental or physical disabilities. The voices of some of these groups have been heard more than others, and the admission of some of them to the status of recognised victims of Nazi persecution took place far later than others, if at all.

Representatives of Roma and Sinti communities became increasingly vocal and active in the course of the 1980s, as did those affected by compulsory sterilisation and euthanasia programmes from the 1990s onwards. Accounts of experiences by forced labourers only began to be elicited by Alexander von Plato and colleagues in a European-wide research team based at the Institute for History and Biography at the Fernuniversität

---

8 See for example Donald L. Niewyk (ed.), *Fresh Wounds: Early Narratives of Holocaust Survival* (Chapel Hill/London: University of North Carolina Press, 1998), 'Introduction', pp. 5-6, about excluding non-standard accounts from the Boder collection. Publications with selections from the HHL collection of essays generally focus on the Jewish stories: Uta Gerhardt and Thomas Karlauf (eds), *The Night of Broken Glass: Eyewitness Accounts of Kristallnacht* (Cambridge: Polity Press, 2012, transl. by Robert Simmons and Nick Somers); Margarete Limberg and Herbert Rübsaat (eds), *Sie durften nicht mehr Deutsche sein: Jüdischer Alltag in Selbstzeugnissen 1933-1938* (Frankfurt/New York: Campus Verlag, 1990), with a reduced selection of these in English translation in Margarete Limberg and Hubert Rübsaat, *Germans no more. Accounts of Jewish Everyday Life, 1933-38* (New York/Oxford: Berghahn, 2006; transl. by Alan Nothnagle); Margarete Limberg and Hubert Rübsaat (eds), *Nach dem 'Anschluss'. Berichte österreichischer EmigrantInnen aus dem Archiv der Harvard University* (Vienna: Mandelbaum Verlag, 2013); Andreas Lixl-Purcell (ed.), *Women of Exile: German-Jewish Autobiographies since* 1933 (Westport, Conn./ London: Greenwood,1988); and Monika Richarz, 'Vorwort' in Monika Richarz (ed.), *Jüdisches Leben in Deutschland: Selbstzeugnisse zur Sozialgeschichte 1918-1945 vol. 3* (Stuttgart: Deutsche Verlags-Anstalt, Leo Baeck Institut, 1982), (pp. 7-12, 1982), p. 9.

(Distance Learning University) Hagen; between 2005 and 2006, some thirty-two projects were carried out in twenty-seven countries.

Gay men, and others who did not fit readily into received categories, generally found far less by way of public interest, and collections of testimony are accordingly sparse. The accounts that began to be published in the 1980s – once homosexuality was no longer a punishable offence in most European countries – generally received little attention; only from the 1990s onwards was this a topic of wider public and professional interest, by which time it was already becoming far too late to solicit survivors' stories on much of a scale, and certainly not on a scale comparable to that of Jewish victims of Nazi persecution.[9] Accounts by survivors such as Pierre Seel in France and Heinz Heger in Austria reveal the continued homophobia and social opprobrium that afflicted them for decades after liberation from Nazi persecution. Their experiences of continued prejudice are painful to read; and it is notable that the major collections of survivor testimony, such as the Yale Fortunoff Archive or the USC Shoah Foundation collection, barely include accounts by gay survivors. People occasionally comment on others who had been imprisoned on charges of homosexuality, or when they recorded

9 But see for example: Claudia Schoppmann, *Days of Masquerade: Life Stories of Lesbians during the Third Reich* (New York: Columbia University Press, 1996); Burkhard Jellonnek, *Homosexuelle unter dem Hakenkreuz: Die Verfolgung von Homosexuellen im Dritten Reich* (Paderborn: Ferdinand Schöningh, 1990); Claudia Schoppmann, 'Zum aktuellen Forschungsstand über lesbische Frauen im Nationalsozalismus', *Invertito. Jahrbuch für die Geschichte der Homosexualitäten* vol. 4, 2002, Special issue: 'Denunziert, verfolgt, ermordet: Homosexuelle Männer und Frauen in der NS-Zeit', pp. 111-116; and for individual accounts, Pierre Seel, *I, Pierre Seel, Deported Homosexual* (New York: Basic Books 2011; orig. French 1994; transl. by Joachim Neugroschel); Heinz Heger, *The Men with the Pink Triangle* (London: Gay Men's Press, transl. David Fernbach, 1980; orig. German 1972).

(frequently unwelcome) advances by other prisoners of the same sex. Memoirs of women who were in the women's concentration camp of Ravensbrück, such as that by Margarete Buber-Neumann, give accounts of lesbian love affairs among prisoners, although this was not the overt reason for their imprisonment.[10] But in general the topic remains marginal.

II. Time and Selfhood

The character of narratives of personal experiences differed, then, in part according to the time of telling. But it differed too for quite personal reasons to do with the individuals themselves, including why they spoke, to whom and about what they were willing to speak, and even – to put it very bluntly – who was still around to do the speaking. Survivors who were already adults at the time of persecution are for simple biological reasons not well represented, if at all, in the huge collections of survivor testimony that took place forty or fifty years later.

The kinds of stories of redemption that have been elicited in the recent 'era of the survivor', emphasising the triumph of the human spirit in adversity, are highly selective in at least two quite different ways: they are not merely produced by those who were young enough at the time of persecution to be still alive and fit enough to give a coherent account many decades later; they are also given by those who had managed to establish and lead sufficiently well-adjusted (even 'successful') lives that they were willing and able to talk about the 'life after' as well as the life before and

10 Margarete Buber-Neumann, *Under Two Dictators: Prisoner of Stalin and Hitler* (London: Random House, Pimlico, 2008; transl. by Edward Fitzgerald; first published 1949).

the experiences during the catastrophe that had overwhelmed them in their youth.

It is therefore not easy for historians to seek to generalise even from the very large collections of survivor testimony. But a few observations may be made about time and selfhood.

Age at the time of Nazi persecution could make a massive difference to subsequent life courses and also the effects on survivors, their attitudes and the ways in which they dealt with the rest of their lives. Let me take an example from the Yale Fortunoff collection. Steven H. and Marion L. were twins who as children survived Bergen-Belsen along with their parents. They were able to make a fresh start in life with a new education beginning on their emigration to the USA after the war. In Bergen-Belsen, they had learnt to count by 'counting corpses'. At the age of nine on arrival in the USA, they had to enter kindergarten to make up for the education they had missed out on in Europe; but they learned English quickly and caught up fast. They suffered physical problems due to years of malnutrition and stunted growth, and had to adjust to a quite different society, but managed this with apparent ease. By contrast, as Marion L. pointed out, their parents had to completely 'start over again' in a foreign country, in a way that was quite different for them as children. Their own parents, Steven H. felt, had a very positive attitude, and became extremely patriotic Americans, impressed with gratitude to their new country. But many of their parents' friends were, as Marion L. describes it, 'so bitter': they 'had lost their spirit' and 'were so angry'; 'they could never make a go of it, they were just crippled human beings'. Even their own mother, despite her positive attitude, had suffered many physical after-effects of her experiences, and, as they put it, 'she's not talking'; she would not 'tell her story'.[11]

The painfulness of memories was not the only reason for not talking; the sense of incommunicability of personal experiences was also significant. Steven H. said he did not talk to his own children about his experiences simply because 'it's pointless'; he also felt that he could not even give his wife 'an appreciation of what it was like'.[12] The topic only came up at home when there was a relevant television programme. Steven's twin sister, Marion L., did give talks in schools, where the students always asked about Anne Frank. But here too she felt there was no way of engaging in a form of communication that would do justice to her own experiences and memories. She could tell the story 'but so much is too private'; moreover, any attempt to talk about redemption and the human spirit, which presumably members of her audiences were expecting, somehow seemed misplaced. In her view, the story should instead be about 'how human beings can do this to other human beings and the tremendous degradation and loss of dignity the people in the camps suffered', as well as the long-term 'peculiarities that are the result of the Holocaust'. Audiences also seemed to assume hierarchies of suffering, with implicit constructions of what it meant to be a 'survivor' and what the standard story 'should' look like – even literally. Steven H. commented jokingly that he felt somewhat 'cheated' when people asked him about having a number on his arm – which as a survivor of Bergen-Belsen rather than Auschwitz he did not. As he put it, 'I really wish I could have had the full course and got this badge of honour'.[13]

11 Steven H. and Marion L., Holocaust Testimony (HVT-544). Fortunoff Video Archive for Holocaust Testimonies, Yale University Library. Interviewed 26 March 1985 by Jaymee Hozer.

12 See Note 11 above.

13 See Note 11 above.

Many survivors who do finally give an account to an interviewer for one of these later collections talk of how their experiences were too painful to want to talk about them; how they wanted to protect their children, and give them a happier childhood and youth than the ones they had themselves had. Mila P. for example was interviewed in 1980 by Dori Laub and Laurel Vlock as one of the earlier interviewees in the Fortunoff Yale project.[14] Born in Chrzanow in 1926, she was a teenager at the time of the German invasion. She had been first deported to Auschwitz, then sent to a labour camp; but a younger sister, aged ten at the time, and both her mother and father, had been killed. Her father was one of six siblings, while her mother was one of seven; no-one from this extended family survived. She later recalled that at first, after the war, there was a phase when 'everyone asked "where were you"'; but later, 'now we know what went on, so nobody really wants to talk about it', as she put it, 'even now' because 'it's too painful'. She had however told her children and other relatives, because she felt it was important for them as members of the wider community: 'As a Jew, they are obligated, they should know'. But for herself, she said, 'I personally don't want to talk about it, because it's too painful, it just goes through me, and I get all upset, nervous and cry.' At the very end of her interview, even with the camera switched off, the sound track continues and she can be heard saying 'And now I feel like I want to die. It's unbelievable.'

Some of these survivors touched on the complex question of 'survivor guilt'. Not everyone felt guilty. Even the twins, Steven H. and Marion L., who had gone through the same experiences and at the same age, differed in their attitude to this question. Marion L. commented that 'You always

14 Mila P., Holocaust Testimony (HVT-111), Fortunoff Video Archive for Holocaust Testimonies, Yale University Library. Interviewed 23 February 1980 by Dori Laub and Laurel Vlock.

feel a little bit guilty, a little bit wondering, about why did you survive, and somehow for the people who are no longer here, you're here – and I do think about that quite a bit'. Her twin brother Steven H., however, was adamantly of a different view: 'survivor guilt, I don't really buy that'. He was, he said, simply glad he had survived: 'no apologies'.[15] But Mila P. was plagued by feelings of guilt: 'Why couldn't my younger sister be alive? She would have been 49 years old today. Why couldn't my parents – why did they have to go with the dead the way they did? What makes me a better person that I survive? It's more like a guilt conscious [*sic*].'[16]

There were other ways in which the character of the uprooting affected people later. Olga S., for example, was a well-educated Czech Jew, born in 1929, who was fluent in a number of languages and came from a relatively wealthy background.[17] On arrival in America after the war, she experienced considerable dissonance between her own self-image and the perception of others that she was just an immigrant with little command of English. It took her quite a while to get over this; and she devoted considerable efforts to becoming as 'American' as she could: as she put it, 'the anxiety of becoming part of our new home was overwhelming'. Her children, born in the USA, had in her view a more difficult time than did the children of other immigrants because 'no matter how hard we tried to become Americanised [...] they sensed it, that there was something different' about being a Jewish survivor. Later, her children became involved in second-generation organisations and activities. In Olga S.'s account, the issues of immigration and settling in a new country seemed

15 See Note 11 above.

16 See Note 14 above.

17 Olga S., Holocaust Testimony (HVT-2705), Fortunoff Video Archive for Holocaust Testimonies, Yale University Library. Interviewed on 4 November 1993 by Naomi Rappaport.

to take priority over memories of bad experiences at the time of persecution; they even, in her interview, seem to overshadow what one might have thought would have been far more traumatic memories, such as the death of her then seven-year-old brother at the hands of the Nazis. She was also quite overwhelmed by her more recent experiences of 'going back' to see the former homes of herself and her husband, who had come from an area quite close to the region where her own family had lived before the war. There, they experienced the expected mixture of curiosity, hostility, and concern about possible requests for return of property. It made Olga S. realise that she had in fact managed to lead a life of some privilege in the USA, quite different from that of her non-Jewish compatriots who had remained in eastern Europe under communism. Seeing her old home and greeted with suspicion by the current inhabitants, she 'then laid it on. Me – come back – to this? Who needs this? Who wants this? We have a wonderful life in the United States [...] It was a sort of vindictiveness actually.' Even so, when pressed finally by the interviewer on her greatest fears at the time, and how she saw things now, she responded that 'the one thing is [...] the deep deep resentment of having uprooted my life.' She did not think her parents or she 'would ever have wanted to go to America'. And, in a sense, she regretted the unlived life: 'As much as I love being here, and I wouldn't change this for anything in the world, there is always this curiosity – no, that isn't really the right word I'm looking for – what would have happened. This was taken away. We didn't come here by choice. And how things would have turned out.' She added: 'I feel comfortable in America', but 'the roots are still there'. The return to see her former home town cured her of ever wanting to return to eastern Europe, but the sense of having had agency in shaping her own life had been taken from her – and she regretted this.

It was not only Jews who experienced disruption in their previous identities and assumed life narratives. Many non-Jews who emigrated no longer felt part of the German society they had left behind. Hildegard W., for example, was born in Berlin in 1912 and in 1931 married a considerably older Jewish man. When the Nazis came to power, she refused to abandon her husband, unlike so many other 'Aryan' partners who dropped their Jewish spouses.[18] They managed eventually to emigrate, and even, after the war, gained some restitution for their lost business as well as, later on, receiving a German pension; as Hildegard W. put it, the Germans 'are very decent now in this respect'. Even so, interviewed in the 1980s following a visit to Germany two or three years earlier, Hildegard W. said of herself that 'you feel as if you don't belong to them any more [...] everything is different [...] strange.' She summarised her experience of older fellow-Germans: 'I don't like them'. Older people almost uniformly told her and her husband that they had known nothing about what had happened, and had not known about the death camps. By contrast she felt younger Germans were different, and were far more interested in hearing about her experiences: 'they wanted to know everything, and felt ashamed [...] couldn't believe it, that their own parents were involved, tried to cover it up, some families'. Her experiences on her visit to Germany in the 1980s are typical of many.

III. Placing the Past
Changing Contexts and the Passage of Generations

This last example brings us to one of the most difficult questions concerning accounts of this period: the roles and self-representations of

---

18 Hildegard W., Holocaust Testimony (HVT-937). Fortunoff Video Archive for Holocaust Testimonies, Yale University Library. Interviewed 14 August 1987 by Laurel Vlock.

perpetrators and people who have been called 'bystanders'; and the relationship between survivor accounts and the wider societies in which they lived after the war.

It may seem a little out of place, when focusing primarily on survivor accounts, to look at the ways in which former perpetrators and those who were complicit in upholding the Nazi system considered and represented their own pasts. But there are a couple of points which are of note here, if we are to understand the changing character, significance and reception of accounts by survivors.

First, changed political circumstances and social relations in different states after the war affected the extent to which former perpetrators were quietly reintegrated into society, effectively rehabilitated, after varying degrees of denazification, potentially punishment, and exclusion. In the three Third Reich successor states – East and West Germany, and Austria – the overwhelming majority of those who had played roles, large and small, in the Nazi machinery of persecution and extermination were never brought to trial for their crimes. Estimates of numbers vary, but between 200,000 and perhaps as many as a million people may have been personally involved in killing Jews. Many more knew about the extermination of Europe's Jews and failed to act; they later pleaded that they had 'known nothing about it'. The reintegration of former Nazi elites and individuals was significant in both West Germany (the Federal Republic of Germany) and Austria, with considerable continuities in the legal professions as well as in significant stretches of the wider civil service. While the structural revolution and turnover of personnel was far greater in communist East Germany (the German Democratic Republic), the medical profession was not radically affected, given the length of training and specialist expertise that was so desperately needed in this area after the war. And in whichever of these states survivors might live, they faced a dominant society of people who had largely been 'fellow travellers' if not more ardent and enthusiastic supporters of the Nazi regime and its leader, Hitler. Innumerable people who had witnessed, benefited from or assisted in the Nazi exploitation and maltreatment of victims now sought as best they could to lead new lives that denied the atrocities of the past.

This was clearly a far less comfortable environment for survivors than other areas might be. But even in a state such as Poland, that had been conquered and occupied by Germany, the environment was on occasion downright hostile. Despite the existence of organisations such as the Central Jewish Historical Commission that collected testimony straight after the war, and despite concerted efforts to collect evidence relating to concentration camps and atrocities and bring perpetrators to court, among the wider public anti-Semitism was rife, pogroms could be violent, and few ordinary Poles were willing to risk losing property they had taken from expropriated Jews. In France, official efforts to restore a semblance of national unity after the divisive shocks of the Vichy period led to an emphasis on resistance and French citizenship, and a consequent tendency to downplay the distinctive character of the persecution of the Jews. Meanwhile, those survivors who had emigrated to Palestine / Israel were initially widely treated with a degree of contempt or suspicion, with critiques of their alleged passivity 'going like lamps to the slaughter' in contrast to the supposed fighting spirit of the Zionist settlers and 'Sabra' who had built up the 'promised land' through physical strength and psycho-logical determination. It was only several decades after the early post-war influx of survivors that they began to be viewed in a more benign light, although the Eichmann trial in 1961 certainly played a role along this path. Even in the USA – where from the late 1970s and 1980s what was now called the Holocaust loomed ever larger – survivors did not necessarily get much of a welcome reception in the early post-war years.

It would take a massive research project to explore systematically the ways in which such differences in broader context affected the kinds of accounts that survivors later gave; but there is little doubt that they were all inflected, in different ways, by the wider context of discourse and discussion. Every account of the past is in some way self-defensive, seeking to construct a version of the self for the consumption of others that is acceptable within a particular normative framework. Moreover, even within any one social and political context there could be cultural shifts over time – many of which were broad, indeed transnational in nature. The shame of being seen to have been passive, of having not demonstrated strength and the courage to fight, would be greater in a context emphasising the virtue of active and organised resistance than it would in a culture that legitimized victimhood and suffering and saw resistance even in the very act of trying to stay alive and maintain one's dignity amidst horrific conditions and while subjected to policies designed specifically to humiliate, dehumanize and degrade their victims.

The growth in receptivity to survivor accounts was rooted in the greater identification of younger generations with victims. And this, as well as growing pressures from particular individuals and groups, finally allowed the emergence and articulation of a wider range of narratives from differing victim groups.

In contrast to the prevalence of 'survivor guilt', there was little evidence of bad consciences on the side of those who sought to cover up their past tracks. While some who had witnessed or participated in atrocities finally started talking more openly and critically about their past – precipitated, for example, by the travelling exhibition on the 'Crimes of the Wehrmacht' from 1995, or the media coverage of debates around Daniel Jonah Goldhagen's book on *Hitler's Willing Executioners*, published the same year – it is also noteworthy that many former soldiers still repeated Nazi interpretations of a 'defensive war'. Similarly, many children of perpetrators either knew little about their fathers' involvement, or found it difficult to face up to the challenges of recognising that a person they loved was also a person whose attitudes and actions they might absolutely have to reject – or risk themselves starting to try to legitimise Nazi crimes. This was a considerable burden on very large numbers of people in the successor states, and one that arguably played a role in the heightened sense of morality and political responsibility that is found in some quarters in Germany today.

Yet for all the efforts subsequent generations have made in 'facing up to the past', perpetrators still remain relatively in the shadows. In remembrance ceremonies, memorial sites and places of suffering across Europe, the focus is primarily on remembering the victims. Many have felt that it would sully such sites of remembrance to mention too much about the perpetrators, those who were responsible for the misery and murder of millions. It is only now, belatedly, as the generations of perpetrators, accomplices and beneficiaries of Nazi crimes are dying out, that more attention is being paid to the depiction of perpetrators in sites of memory.

Conclusions

Where has this brief survey of aspects of the personal impact of Nazi persecution taken us, and what conclusions can we draw?

From such a vast field, with such a wealth of personal material, it is difficult to make generalisations. But it is clear that the context of telling one's story mattered greatly; and that later contexts made a big difference to the kinds of stories that were elicited and heard. It is also clear that while any experience of persecution at the hands of the Nazis had a personal impact, later evaluations of degrees of suffering or the kinds of responses also played a role in how people felt about themselves. Only once we can address the wider questions of context as well as the individual psychologies of those who lived through these times will we begin to attain a better understanding of the full impact of the catastrophe that engulfed so many people under Nazi rule.

* * * * * * *

Yearbook of the Research Centre for German and Austrian Exile Studies

'.... a must-read for anyone interested in the field of Exile Studies in Britain and internationally.' (*Modern Language Review*, 2005)

Exile and Gender I (Vol. 17)

eds. **Charmian Brinson** and **Andrea Hammel**

ISBN 9789004313798 x, 251pp Eur 99,00

This volume focuses on the work of exiled women writers and journalists as well as on gendered representations in the writing of both male and female exiled writers. The seventeen contributions (in English and German) set out to celebrate and critically examine the concepts of gender and sexuality in exile in a wide range of texts by well-known and lesser known authors, and throw light on many different aspects of gendered authorship and gendered relations, whilst also looking at two bibliographic rarities: exile newspapers intended for and directed at a female readership.

Contributors: Hiltrud Arens; Montserrat Bascoy Lamelas; Wiebke von Bernstorff; Charmian Brinson; Rosa Maria Gómez Pato; Andrea Hammel; Birgit Maier-Katkin; Aine McGillicuddy; Katharina Prager; Esther Saletta; Rose Sillars; Jörg Thunecke; Christine Ujma; Trinidad Marín Villora; Benedikt Wolf; Amira Zmiric; Veronika Zwerger.

Volumes can be purchased direct from the Brill online shop at http://www.brill.com/

Other Forthcoming Titles

Foreign Parts

German and Austrian Actors on the British Stage 1933-1960

by **Richard Dove**

Foreign Parts offers a case study in Anglo-German relations in the theatre. How British was the British theatre during and after the Second World War? This book tells the unique story of five German-speaking actors (Lucie Mannheim, Frederick Valk, Gerhard Hinze/ Gerard Heinz, Lilly Kann and Martin Miller) who, after arriving as refugees from Nazi Germany, made the transition to the British stage in a period of heightened nationalism before and during World War II. While the emotional intensity of their performances won the applause of audiences and the approval of critics, their success also depended on the support of British theatre personalities – from Alec Clunes and Tyrone Guthrie to actors Sybil Thorndike and John Gielgud. The book also recounts their role in British propaganda broadcasts to Germany, including Martin Miller's satirical impersonation of his fellow-Austrian Adolf Hitler and Lucie Mannheim's anti-Nazi version of the popular hit *Lilli Marlene*.

Richard Dove is Emeritus Professor of German at the University of Greenwich and the author of various books on German-speaking exile in Britain.

Cambridge: MHRA [Legenda]

ISBN 978-1-78188-473-7

Der Ritt über 'n Bodensee: Erinnerungen einer Schauspielerin by Lilly Kann

edited and introduced by

Charmian Brinson and **Richard Dove**

The memoirs of German Jewish actress Lilly Kann (1893-1976), describe her life and work in the theatre, both in pre-emigration Germany, and in Britain after her emigration in 1939. They present the reader with a double slice of German and British theatrical history between which Kann draws many perceptive and first-hand comparisons, and include depictions of two particularly noteworthy periods in her career: firstly, after Hitler's assumption of power, the six years she spent working at the *Jüdischer Kulturbund* in Berlin; and secondly, the period immediately following her emigration when she acted in the lively refugee theatres of North London, the *Kleine Bühne* of the *Freier Deutscher Kulturbund* and the *Laterndl* of the Austrian Centre. The volume (in German) comprises an edited version of the memoirs together with a biographical/historical introduction by the editors and biographical notes on many of the German and British actors, directors and other theatre people with whom Lilly Kann worked.

Charmian Brinson is Emeritus Professor of German at Imperial College London. Richard Dove is Emeritus Professor of German at the University of Greenwich. Both are the authors of various books on German-speaking exile in Britain.

Berne: Peter Lang [Exildokumente]

ISBN 978-3-0343-2593-6